UNLOCKING POTENTIAL

Unlocking Potential

5 Ways to Outsmarting Life's Challenges

Inner Power

Inner Strength Counselling

CONTENTS

1 - Your Attitude As A Trusted Ally 1

2 - Positive Thinking 18

3 - Innovative Thinking – Cognitive
Restructuring 40

4 - Creative Thinking 57

5 - The Art Of Problem-Solving 73

1

YOUR ATTITUDE AS A TRUSTED ALLY

The way you approach life has an impact, on every aspect of it. To find success and happiness it's important to have an attitude that supports you.

Your attitude can be seen in your behavior and the things that happen to you. The Law of Attraction suggests that what you put out into the world comes back, to you. So the trick is to make your attitude work in your favor by making it your ally.

To effectively make your attitude your ally, it's imperative to understand its significance. Learning how to cultivate a positive attitude and integrating this concept into your daily life is essential.

While transforming your attitude into an ally requires effort, the investment is worthwhile. Your attitude has the power to shape your entire life, and by allowing it to guide you, you can bring about positive changes in every aspect of your current situation.

What Do You Mean Your Attitude is a Trusted Ally?

"Embracing your attitude as your ally" means that your attitude plays a role, in shaping the direction you take in life. Essentially your attitude is reflected in your actions, thoughts, and interactions ultimately determining the path you follow. In this context, an ally refers to the journey itself. It is guided by your attitude.

To cultivate your attitude as an ally it is important to recognize that it encompasses how you behave think and treat others—having an impact on every aspect of your life. Making a choice to adopt an attitude is crucial in shaping your ally into a positive path. Your attitude holds power in influencing how you perceive things and how others respond to you.

Deciding to make your attitude your ally involves making choices between positivity and negativity or hard work and laziness. The chosen mindset has an impact, on the outcomes you experience in life. While embracing an attitude does not guarantee perfection in everything it enhances your ability to focus on the aspects of situations making the environment seem more favorable.

A positive attitude fosters self-belief and empowerment, enabling you to set and achieve goals without being hindered by negative energy. Its influence extends beyond individual well-being; it shapes the people and circumstances around you. The impact of a positive attitude is potent and evident.

In the quest for a fulfilling life, the choice becomes evident – most people naturally gravitate toward positivity, desiring a life characterized by happiness and smooth flow. However, to manifest these positive outcomes, it's essential to consciously make your positive attitude your ally. This involves aligning your actions, thoughts, and lifestyle with positivity, ensuring that your attitude becomes a driving force toward the desired positive path in life.

How to Make Your Attitude an Ally

Making your attitude your ally involves recognizing and harnessing the power of a positive mindset to influence your life positively. Here are steps to make your attitude your ally:

Believe in the Influence of a Positive Attitude:
  - Acknowledge that your attitude plays a crucial role in shaping your life and outcomes.

Shift Your Thinking:
  - Change any skepticism about positive thinking

by actively shifting your mindset towards believing that a positive attitude leads to positive results.

Look for Proof:
- Seek evidence that supports the idea that positive attitudes yield positive outcomes. Observe the positive influences around you.

Experiment with Positivity:
- Dedicate a day to maintaining a positive attitude. Observe how others respond to you and note any positive changes in your interactions and experiences.

Convince Yourself:
- Once you witness the positive impact of your attitude, convince yourself that maintaining a positive outlook genuinely influences your life.

Sustain the Positive Attitude:
- Continuously cultivate and sustain a positive attitude in your daily life. Let it become a guiding force.

Incorporate Positive Thinking:
- Apply positive thinking to your thoughts, ideas, actions, body language, and goals. Actively turn negative thoughts into positive ones.

Train Your Thoughts:

- Train yourself to instinctively find the positive in any situation. Consistently redirect negative thoughts towards positive perspectives.

Positive Body Language:
- Ensure that your body language reflects positivity. Keep your body open, make eye contact, and avoid closed gestures like crossing your arms. A smile is a powerful positive body language.

Align Body Language with Words:
- Ensure that your body language aligns with your words to convey authenticity and sincerity.

Set Positive Goals:
- Establish positive goals for yourself. Goals provide direction and purpose, and positive goals contribute to maintaining a positive attitude.

Maintain Consistency:
- Consistently uphold your positive attitude, letting it guide your actions and decisions.

By consciously incorporating these steps into your life, you actively make your attitude your ally, allowing positivity to influence your thoughts, behaviors, and experiences.

Definition of a Positive Attitude

Positive Attitude Checklist:

To ensure your attitude is consistently positive, consider the following characteristics of a positive person:

Upbeat and Cheerful:
- Maintain a positive and optimistic demeanor.

Optimistic Outlook:
- View situations with a focus on possibilities, seeing the glass as half full rather than half empty.

Finds Beauty Everywhere:
- Recognize and appreciate the beauty in various aspects of life.

Emphasizes the Good:
- Prioritize positive aspects over negative ones in any situation.

Love for Life:
- Approach life with genuine love and enthusiasm.

Avoids Negative Words:
- Use positive language and refrain from negativity.

Sense of Playfulness:
- Embrace a lighthearted and fun-loving attitude.

Respects Others:
- Refrain from putting others down and show genuine respect.

Caring Nature:
- Demonstrate sincere concern and care for those around you.

Contributor to Others' Well-being:
- Actively seek ways to improve the lives of others.

Giving, Not Taking:
- Embrace a mindset of giving and contributing rather than focusing on personal gain.

Non-Hurtful Behavior:
- Avoid actions or words that may cause harm to others.

Solution-Oriented:
- Focus on finding solutions rather than dwelling on problems.

Goal-Oriented:

- Demonstrate a willingness to work towards and achieve goals.

If these traits align with your behavior, you are likely to embody a positive attitude. If not, consider incorporating these characteristics into your daily life to shape yourself into a more positive person. Strive to embody each aspect of this checklist, fostering a genuinely positive and uplifting approach to life.

Positive Living Tips

Create a Happy Place:
- Develop a mental sanctuary where you can retreat when feeling stressed or down, providing relaxation and joy.

Adopt a Hobby:
- Engage in activities you enjoy to uplift your spirits and maintain a positive attitude.

Incorporate Exercise:
- Embrace a regular exercise routine, recognizing its positive impact on both physical and mental well-being.

Use Affirmations:

- Integrate positive sayings, verses, or quotes into your daily routine to instantly boost your attitude.

Explore New Things:
 - Approach the unknown with curiosity rather than avoidance.

Accept Challenges:
 - Embrace challenges, seeking creative ways to overcome them and grow.

Embrace Messiness:
 - Allow yourself the freedom to make messes and learn, recognizing that happiness can be messy and liberating.

Challenge Conventional Rules:
 - Occasionally defy rules and authority, finding excitement and a sense of freedom in breaking norms.

Immerse Yourself in Pretend Play:
 - Tap into your imagination, escape from reality, and pretend to be someone else, fostering enjoyment and smiles.

Remember, these tips serve as a foundation, and you can customize them based on your preferences and what brings you joy. Identify the activities and experiences that genuinely make you happy, and allow them to guide you toward cultivating a more positive attitude.

Your Attitude is Your Trusted Ally

It's seemingly straightforward to make your attitude your ally, and the prospect is undoubtedly worth a try. If you're accustomed to letting your attitude lead you, the concept is familiar. However, many unintentionally let negative attitudes become their allies, often more prevalent than positive ones.

Negativity tends to draw more attention than positivity, contributing to a world inundated with pessimistic attitudes. Reflecting on your life, you may identify instances where negativity influenced outcomes, emphasizing the need to shift toward a positive attitude.

Remember a time when negativity impacted a situation? Even if the circumstances weren't inherently positive, a negative attitude likely exacerbated the challenges. This underscores the importance of cultivating a positive mindset.

To truly make your attitude your ally, focus on training your mind to find the positive in everything. Ignore the negative or transform it into a positive, ensuring your ally isn't cluttered with detrimental influences.

Imagine your attitude as an ally. A positive ally is unobstructed, facilitating a smoother journey through life. Conversely, a negative ally hinders progress, requiring effort to navigate roadblocks. Thus, the choice is clear: a positive attitude paves the way for an easier, more fulfilling life.

Transforming your attitude into a positive ally involves reshaping your daily activities, interactions, thoughts, and goals. Consciously maintain positivity in your thoughts and goals, as this profoundly influences your attitude.

Interactions with others are key broadcasts of your attitude. Approaching people with positivity elicits positive responses. For instance, a job interview conducted with a positive attitude enhances your chances of success. Your daily interactions significantly impact your life; ensure they emanate positivity.

Developing a routine of positive thinking takes time and effort. Initially, you'll need to work hard to infuse positivity into every aspect of your life. Resist negative thoughts and actions, fostering a positive approach even in challenging situations.

Approaching life with positivity often leads to positive experiences. People are more inclined to assist and support you when approached with positivity. Thus, your attitude as an ally opens doors to numerous positive outcomes.

Using your attitude as your ally transcends individual moments; it's about enveloping your life in positivity. Surround yourself with positive people, seek positive situations, and immerse yourself in uplifting experiences. Eliminate negativity to pave your road with positivity, ensuring positive results along the way.

What Can Your Trusted Ally Do For You?

Adopting a positive attitude and embracing it as your ally is a transformative journey that yields immediate and noticeable changes, particularly if you're transitioning from a negative mindset. This shift in perspective has multifaceted impacts on your life.

People will respond more positively to you as you exude optimism. A simple smile can elicit a positive response, illustrating the tangible effects of a positive attitude in interpersonal interactions.

Beyond social interactions, your positive attitude will empower you to perceive the good in everything. Regardless of life's challenges, you'll navigate them without succumbing to anger or depression, fundamentally altering your outlook on life.

Handling adversity becomes more manageable as your positive attitude guides you through problems and difficult situations. The transformation may extend deeper than expected, influencing habits such as smoking. If stress or relaxation triggers your smoking habit, a positive attitude might help you quit by addressing the root causes.

By making your attitude your ally, you'll no longer rely on addictions to cope with stress, as your newfound positivity will guide you through challenges. Quitting habits like smoking becomes achievable without the psychological need for substances.

Your positive attitude becomes a powerful force, attracting positivity into your life. The shift is palpable; positive influences and experiences gravitate toward you. The magnetic effect of a positive attitude may seem extraordinary, shaping a life that reflects the optimistic energy you project.

Interpretations of how a positive attitude works can vary—some may view it through the lens of karma, believing that what you project returns to you. Others may see it as a mental phenomenon, where thinking positively begets positive outcomes. Regardless of the interpretation, the impact of making your attitude your ally is undeniable.

In essence, making your attitude your ally is a winning proposition, transforming your life in ways that resonate with your beliefs and personal philosophy. The power of this shift becomes evident once implemented, underscoring the profound influence a positive attitude can have on the trajectory of your life.

Here Comes an Example

Emma's life was engulfed in pessimism—high blood pressure, no close friends, a disliked job, and mounting debt. Until she stumbled upon the idea of making her attitude her ally. Skeptical but desperate for change, Emma decided to give it a shot.

The next morning, Emma consciously replaced her negative thoughts with positive ones. Instead of dreading the daily traffic jam, she focused on her favorite morning song, appreciating the simple joy it brought. She greeted co-workers, chatted with the secretary, and, to her surprise, received acknowledgment from her boss for her recent project.

Seizing the opportunity to make her attitude her ally, Emma's boss recognized her positive shift and saw her potential for a management position. Emma's promotion marked the beginning of a positive transformation in her life.

Embracing this newfound positivity, Emma made friends at work, elevated her self-esteem, and experienced a life she once only dreamed of. Her story serves as a testament to the power of making your attitude your ally.

Analyzing Emma's situation reveals the profound impact of this change. Previously, stuck in traffic, Emma's negativity prevented her from appreciating her favorite song. By choosing positivity, she not only enjoyed the music but also experienced a boost in mood, contributing to her overall well-being.

Moreover, Emma's shift from isolation to socializing at work had cascading effects. Building relationships improved her workplace satisfaction, and her boss noticed her, eventually leading to a promotion she wouldn't have considered in her previous mindset.

In just one day, Emma made significant changes that altered the trajectory of her life. Her story illustrates the potential for impactful transformation through a shift in attitude. The positive ripple effects on her health, relationships, and career highlight the tangible benefits of making her attitude your ally.

Emma's experience is a compelling narrative, encouraging others to consider making this change in their lives, knowing that, like her, they have nothing to lose and everything to gain.

Conclusion

Now that you've grasped the concept of making your attitude your ally and learned how to integrate it into your life, you can undoubtedly recognize its value as an idea worth testing.

The concepts outlined here provide a solid starting point for making your attitude your ally. Transforming your attitude into a positive force is a straightforward process.

Once you commit to this change, nothing can hinder you from enjoying the benefits of a positive attitude serving as your ally. It all begins with that crucial first step.

Commitment is key. You must dedicate yourself to the process, pledging to become a positive person.

Establish a goal to infuse positivity into your attitude and let it guide you.

Goals wield significant power, motivating and propelling you toward accomplishment. Set a goal to foster a positive attitude, ensuring your newfound positivity becomes your ally.

Recall the impact of making your attitude your ally:

- It shapes your perspective toward life positively.
- It enables you to face challenges and adversity with newfound resilience.
- It aids in stress reduction.
- It empowers you to influence others positively.
- It facilitates personal transformation.
- It initiates a newfound appreciation for life.

Keep Emma's story in mind to maintain your commitment to this positive transformation. Let her experiences remind you that positive outcomes can stem from this effort.

Armed with a deep understanding of what making your attitude your ally entails, you're now in control. No one can compel you to embrace positivity, nor can they force your attitude to become your ally.

Considering all you've learned, can you genuinely pass up the opportunity to enhance your life significantly? Wouldn't you want to explore the potential greatness your life could attain?

With the knowledge you now possess, can you comfortably live without at least attempting this transformative journey?

You may find yourself increasingly excited about the possibilities of a positive attitude in the coming days. Subconsciously, change will begin, making it too compelling to dismiss what you've learned.

You're on the path to making your attitude your ally effortlessly. Soon, you'll start reaping the rewards. So, why wait? Commence the journey to making your attitude your ally today. Shed the negativity, wear a smile, and radiate positivity to everyone around you.

Apply the valuable tips and advice accumulated here. Make your attitude your ally, instigate change in your life, become a better person, and inspire positive living in those around you. Transform into a role model, realizing your full potential.

You stand to lose nothing and gain everything by fostering a positive attitude. So, embrace positivity now, and let your positive attitude become your unwavering ally. Once you experience this change, you'll never want to return to the confines of negative thinking.

2

POSITIVE THINKING

You've likely encountered the advice to think positively during challenging times. This suggestion is rooted in the widely embraced belief in the power of positive thinking.

The notion that positive energy can be contagious, influencing others to reciprocate with positivity, is widely accepted. It revolves around the idea that what you emit into the world will eventually return to you.

Positive influences surround us because people naturally gravitate toward feeling good. In most cases, individuals prefer positivity over negativity. This preference is relatable; being around someone who exudes optimism and energy is generally more appealing than being in the company of someone who appears gloomy and disheartened.

Recognizing that positive thinking and a positive

attitude can significantly impact one's life, people are inclined to incorporate these principles. The potency of positive thinking is profound, and by actively embracing it, you can unlock a multitude of positive benefits in your life.

What is Positive Thinking?

Positive thinking is characterized by adopting optimistic thoughts and focusing on the bright side of situations. It involves eliminating negative thoughts and actively seeking the positive aspects in every circumstance. A positive thinker consistently strives to find something good in various situations.

In life, positive thinking plays a significant role. Individuals who cultivate a positive mindset generally experience a more positive life compared to those who lean towards negativity. Positive thinkers can maintain an upbeat demeanor regardless of the situation because they choose not to dwell on the negative aspects. Instead, they actively seek positive elements and solutions in challenging situations.

When faced with adversity, positive thinkers do not allow themselves to succumb to negativity; rather, they focus on finding positive aspects and solutions to overcome obstacles. Their attitude differs markedly from that of negative thinkers. Positive individuals endeavor to stay cheerful, and energized, and avoid sinking into feelings of fatigue or lethargy. They take proactive steps to uplift themselves.

The application of positive thinking extends to various facets of life, from minor occurrences to major life events. It serves as a valuable tool during challenging times and can enhance the quality of an average day.

Positive thinking empowers individuals to identify the silver lining even in unfavorable situations. It equips them to replace negative thoughts with constructive ones.

By embracing positive thinking, individuals can break the pattern of defaulting to negative responses when faced with challenges. It enables them to anticipate favorable outcomes and project an attitude conducive to attracting positive experiences.

Positive thinking is transformative, allowing individuals to convert negatives into positives. It encourages adopting a brighter perspective on life, opening up new possibilities and creating a more optimistic and powerful vision of one's future. Through positive thinking, individuals can unlock the door to a life filled with positivity and success.

How is Positive Thinking Useful?

The power of positive thinking is undeniably transformative, impacting individuals on personal, interpersonal, and environmental levels. Its influence manifests in three significant ways: shaping personal attitude, affecting those around you, and even influencing your surroundings.

Personal Attitude:

Positive thinking profoundly affects your general attitude. As you incorporate positive thinking into your life, you'll undergo a shift in perspective. Your outlook on life becomes more optimistic, allowing you to discover the good in situations. This change in mindset promotes happiness and resilience. Positive thinking becomes a guiding force, steering you away from negative thoughts and leading you toward a brighter, more uplifting mental state.

Influence on Others:

The impact of positive thinking extends to those around you. Your positive attitude becomes palpable, influencing the way people interact with you. Others will likely treat you with kindness and attentiveness, reflecting the positivity you exude. You may notice improvements in how people engage with you, displaying acts of kindness, offering help, and even adopting a more positive attitude themselves. The contagious nature of positivity means that your optimism can inspire those around you to embrace a more positive mindset.

Environmental Influence:

Positive thinking has a subtle yet profound effect

on your environment. While it doesn't guarantee that everything will go perfectly, it alters your perception. Positive thinkers are less likely to dwell on negatives, enabling them to appreciate the small joys in life. This heightened awareness of positive elements in your surroundings contributes to an overall positive environment. You start noticing the beauty in little things, fostering a more optimistic and fulfilling experience of your surroundings.

Positive thinking empowers you to believe in yourself and your capabilities. By eliminating negative thoughts, you create space for self-assurance and confidence. This newfound belief in your abilities allows you to set and achieve goals without the hindrance of self-doubt.

To harness the power of positive thinking, it requires conscious effort and commitment. When negative thoughts arise, actively redirect them toward positive perspectives. Train yourself to seek the positive in any situation, fostering a habit that gradually shapes your overall attitude.

The undeniable power of positive thinking lies in its ability to shape your life profoundly. Its contagious nature spreads beyond personal boundaries, influencing the world around you. Embracing positive thinking enables you to live life to its fullest potential, navigating challenges with resilience and savoring the richness of positive experiences. It becomes a guiding force that empowers you to embrace life without letting negativity impede your journey.

Your Body Language Shows It

Body language, comprising movements, gestures, and facial expressions, is a powerful communicator of emotions and attitudes. It often conveys messages beyond what words express, and aligning it with positive thinking is crucial for effective communication and interactions.

Alignment of Body Language with Positive Thinking:

When cultivating positive thinking, it's essential to synchronize your body language with your mindset. A genuine commitment to positive thinking naturally reflects in your body language. Conversely, incongruent body language might betray your true feelings, even if your words convey positivity. Being conscious of your body language is integral to presenting a consistent and authentic positive image.

Understanding the Impact of Body Language:

Learning about body language enhances your ability to recognize and control it. Negative body language can undermine positive thinking, so being aware of non-verbal cues is essential. For instance, crossed arms or averted eye contact might convey defensiveness or discomfort, potentially contradicting a positive message.

The Power of a Smile:

A smile is a universal and powerful positive body language signal. When you smile at someone, it often elicits a reciprocal smile. This small gesture can create a ripple effect, spreading positivity. A smile communicates happiness, openness, and a willingness to connect. Integrating smiles into your interactions contributes to a positive atmosphere and influences the mood of those around you.

Contagious Nature of Positive Body Language:

Positive body language, much like positive thinking, is contagious. Approaching situations with a cheerful demeanor and open body language tends to foster positive experiences. People are more inclined to assist and cooperate when met with positive non-verbal cues. Being mindful of your body language ensures that you radiate positivity, influencing the dynamics of your interactions.

Avoiding Negative Body Language:

Recognizing and avoiding negative body language is a crucial aspect of aligning your non-verbal cues with positive thinking. Negative body language, such as slouching, crossed arms, or lack of eye contact, can convey disinterest or resistance. Consistent effort is required to replace these habits with positive alternatives that reinforce your positive mindset.

The Integration of Positive Thinking and Positive Body Language:

In the journey of positive thinking, the integration of positive body language is transformative. It's not merely about wearing a positive mask; it's about embodying positivity in every aspect. Positive body language becomes an extension of your optimistic mindset, reinforcing your commitment to a positive way of life.

In conclusion, positive body language is a significant component of positive thinking. Being mindful of your non-verbal cues, understanding their impact, and aligning them with your positive mindset contribute to more authentic and influential communication. As you cultivate positive thinking, let your body language speak the language of positivity, creating a harmonious and uplifting environment for yourself and those around you.

The Adversary of Positive Thinking

While negative thoughts may seem like the primary adversary of positive thinking, the real saboteur is the art of making excuses. Excuses are subtle tactics the mind employs to avoid taking responsibility, and they can significantly hinder the development of a positive mindset.

The Deceptive Nature of Excuses:

Excuses serve as a camouflage for negative thoughts, disguising them as justifications or reasons. When you make an excuse, you're essentially deflecting responsibility and allowing negativity to seep in. It's a subtle form of self-sabotage, as excuses provide a false sense of reassurance while perpetuating negative thought patterns.

Excuses and Negative Thoughts:

Excuses often pave the way for negative thoughts to linger. By making excuses, you're creating a mental loophole that allows negativity to persist. Rather than addressing challenges or setbacks head-on, excuses offer a convenient escape, preventing the cultivation of a positive outlook.

Identifying Excuses:

Being aware of the excuses you make is crucial in the journey toward positive thinking. Excuses can manifest in various forms, such as blaming external factors, downplaying your abilities, or justifying inaction. When you catch yourself making an excuse, it's an opportunity to pause and reflect on the real motives behind it.

Breaking the Excuse Habit:

Overcoming the habit of making excuses is essential for fostering a positive mindset. It requires conscious effort and self-reflection. Instead of resorting to excuses, challenge yourself to confront situations directly. Ask yourself why you feel the need to make an excuse and what underlying negative thoughts you might be avoiding.

Awareness as a Weapon Against Excuses:

The power to overcome excuses lies in awareness. By being mindful of the excuses you make, you can interrupt the cycle of negative thinking. When faced with challenges, acknowledge them without immediately seeking an excuse. This shift in mindset is pivotal for nurturing positivity and resilience.

Persistence in Positive Thinking:

It's normal to encounter moments where excuses seem like a tempting way out. However, persistence is key. Understand that excuses only provide temporary relief, and the long-term impact on your positive thinking is detrimental. Choose to face challenges directly, and gradually, the habit of making excuses will lose its grip on your mindset.

Embracing Responsibility:

Positive thinking thrives in an environment of responsibility. Instead of making excuses, take ownership of your thoughts, actions, and reactions. Accepting responsibility empowers you to navigate challenges with a positive mindset, fostering personal growth and resilience.

In conclusion, the battle against negative thinking involves confronting the true adversary: excuses. By dismantling the habit of making excuses, you pave the way for genuine positive thinking. Cultivate awareness, persist in facing challenges directly, and embrace responsibility – these actions will fortify your journey toward a more positive and empowered mindset.

Activating the Force of Positive Thinking in Your Everyday Life

Training Your Mind for Positive Thinking: A Lifestyle Shift

Shifting from a negative mindset to positive thinking is a transformative journey that requires conscious effort and commitment. It involves training your mind to embrace positivity, even when faced with challenges. Here are some strategies to make positive thinking a natural part of your life:

Immerse Yourself in Positive Content:

Surround yourself with positive influences. Read books, articles, or quotes that inspire optimism. Seek out motivational speakers or podcasts. Immerse yourself in content that reinforces positive thinking and uplifts your spirit.

Visualization for Positive Imagery:
Use the power of visualization to picture yourself acting, thinking, and feeling positive. Create mental images of success, happiness, and accomplishment. Visualization helps align your thoughts with positive outcomes, reinforcing a proactive mindset.

Embrace Positive Language:
Choose your words carefully, both in your internal dialogue and external communication. Replace negative words with positive ones. Your language influences your thoughts, and positive words contribute to fostering an optimistic outlook.

Radiate Positivity Through Smiles:
A simple smile can convey positivity to yourself and others. Make a conscious effort to smile more often. Even during challenging times, a smile can help shift your perspective and contribute to a positive atmosphere.

Persistence and Consistency:
Positive thinking requires ongoing effort. Be persistent and consistent in your commitment to positivity. Don't let a single day pass without actively

engaging in positive thoughts and actions. Over time, this consistency will reshape your mindset.

Identify and Address Negative Thoughts:
Be mindful of negative thoughts when they arise. Understand their origins and challenge them constructively. Recognizing negative thinking is the first step toward replacing it with positive alternatives.

Overcome Fears Through Positive Thinking:
Identify and confront fears that contribute to negative thinking. Often, fears lose their power when faced directly. Trust in yourself and your ability to handle challenges, gradually diminishing the impact of fear on your mindset.

Monitor and Channel Emotions:
Pay attention to your emotions and strive to channel them in positive directions. Focus on feelings of happiness, success, and strength. Minimize emotions like fear, self-doubt, and weakness by consciously steering your thoughts.

Surround Yourself With Happiness:
Engage in activities that bring joy and happiness. Watch uplifting movies, read inspirational books, or listen to cheerful music. Surrounding yourself with positivity enhances your overall emotional well-being.

Choose Positive Company:

Surround yourself with individuals who share a positive outlook. Avoid people who consistently exhibit negative behavior or engage in pessimistic conversations. A positive company can reinforce and support your journey toward positive thinking.

Set Goals for Positive Change:

Establish realistic goals aligned with positive thinking. Goals provide direction and motivation. Work towards achieving these goals, using them as benchmarks for your progress in cultivating a positive mindset.

Readiness for Change:

Assess your readiness for a positive thinking lifestyle. Reflect on whether you are truly prepared to let go of negativity, embrace optimism, and put in the effort required for this transformation. Commitment is crucial for lasting change.

Goal Setting for Positive Transformation:

Set specific goals related to positive thinking. Outline steps to gradually integrate positive thinking into your daily life. Setting and achieving these goals will reinforce your commitment and contribute to the evolution of a positive mindset.

In conclusion, positive thinking is not an overnight

transformation but a lifestyle shift that requires dedication and persistence. By actively incorporating these strategies into your daily routine, you can train your mind to embrace positivity and navigate life's challenges with optimism.

The Impact of Positive Thinking

Positive thinking is a force that has the potential to profoundly impact your life, bringing about transformative changes and shaping your reality. As you integrate positive thinking into your daily existence, you'll witness its remarkable effects in various aspects of your life.

Positive Thinking as a Lifestyle:

Embracing positive thinking is not just a one-time decision; it's a commitment to a new lifestyle. As you immerse yourself in positive thoughts and attitudes, you'll experience a gradual shift in your mindset.

Positive Thinking's Impact on Emotions:

The power of positive thinking extends to your emotional well-being. You'll find yourself waking up with a sense of happiness and optimism. Over time, feelings of sadness will diminish, and you'll navigate your day with an upbeat attitude, regardless of external circumstances.

Influence on Interpersonal Relationships:

Positive thinking has a contagious quality. Those around you will notice the change in your demeanor. People will respond with positive words and actions, and your optimistic attitude will become a source of inspiration for others.

Enhanced Problem-Solving Abilities:
Adopting positive thinking equips you with better coping mechanisms. When faced with challenges, you won't succumb to despair but will actively seek positive aspects to focus on. This newfound perspective makes navigating difficulties more manageable.

Handling Adversity with Resilience:
Positive thinking strengthens your resilience in the face of adversity. Instead of falling apart when confronted with difficulties, you'll approach setbacks with a positive mindset. The ability to see beyond challenges makes overcoming them a smoother process.

A Shift in Perspective:
The lens through which you view life will undergo a transformation. Fear of the unknown will be replaced with a sense of anticipation and enjoyment for learning and conquering new challenges. Positive thinking enables you to embrace life with a newfound optimism.

Positive Thinking as a Catalyst:

Your positive mindset will serve as a catalyst for change. You'll notice that what once seemed impossible now becomes achievable. Positive thinking opens doors to opportunities and propels you toward goals you may have doubted before.

Reshaping Your Life:

The cumulative effect of positive thinking is a complete reshaping of your life. It allows you to live authentically, accomplishing more than you thought possible. The once-unattainable becomes within reach, and your life transforms in ways you had only dreamed of.

Embracing the Possible:

Positive thinking challenges the notion of impossibility. What may have seemed crazy or far-fetched becomes not only believable but attainable. By altering the way you perceive challenges and opportunities, positive thinking paves the way for the realization of your goals.

Belief in the Power of Positive Thinking:

Embark on a transformative journey as you integrate positive thinking into your daily routine and witness its profound impact. Positive thinking isn't just a mindset; it's a force that can reshape your entire existence.

As you welcome positive thinking into your life, you'll experience a noticeable shift. Your days will commence with a sense of joy and optimism, gradually replacing any lingering feelings of sadness. Before long, happiness will become your default state, regardless of the challenges life throws your way.

The ripple effect of your positive mindset will extend to your interactions with others. You'll find yourself greeted with positivity, and your optimistic attitude will prove contagious, influencing those around you. Navigating challenging situations will become second nature, as you focus on the positive aspects to guide you through.

Your perspective on life will undergo a profound transformation. No longer will you fear the unknown; instead, you'll embrace it, relishing the opportunity to learn and conquer new challenges.

It may sound improbable that a mere shift in thinking can revolutionize your life, but the power of positive thinking is undeniable. Prepare to witness the incredible changes it can bring, making the impossible not only possible but a tangible reality in your life. Embrace the strength and effectiveness of positive thinking to live the life you've always dreamed of."While it might sound incredible that a shift in thinking can lead to such profound changes, the belief in the power of positive thinking is grounded in its demonstrated effectiveness. The positive transformation experienced by individuals attests to the strength of this mindset.

In conclusion, positive thinking is not merely a concept; it is a dynamic force that has the potential to reshape your life. As you integrate positive thinking into your daily routine, its effects will permeate every aspect of your existence, bringing about positive changes that once may have seemed unattainable. The power of positive thinking is not just a belief but a reality waiting to be experienced.

Here Comes an Example

Alex was in the middle of a very nasty divorce. His soon-to-be ex-wife was fighting him all the way about everything possible. He had trouble sleeping, and eating and felt himself slipping into a great depression.

Every time he had to meet with his attorney, he experienced stomach pains and he was sure he was getting an ulcer. He was constantly worried about being able to make it after the divorce was finalized. He also worried about how this all was affecting his two children.

Alex was in a very bad place. Then, one day, he ran across some information about the power of positive thinking. He was so interested in what he read that he decided to see if it could work in his life.

Alex started to become aware of his thoughts. He

started to push all the negative thoughts out of his mind.

Instead of approaching his situation with fear, he went towards it with courage. He stood his ground and did not give in. He laid down his demands and stuck to them. He stopped letting himself be walked all over by his ex.

Alex began thinking positively about his situation. He began envisioning a positive outcome. He stopped letting himself get down about what was happening in his life and started looking at all the positive things he had gotten out of it.

Now that he was separated, he felt happier. He could do whatever he wanted without having his ex nag him. He was closer than ever to his kids because he now cherished the limited time he was able to spend with them. He was able to get his financial affairs in order, too.

Alex was able to get through the divorce. He came out in the end without losing everything, being able to maintain a good relationship with his kids and even being able to somehow maintain a civil relationship with his ex.

By changing to a positive attitude, he was able to stop letting everything get him down. He was able to get through the trying situation without letting himself fall apart. In the end, the power of positive thinking was working for Alex, just as it can work for you.

You can see through Alex's story that positive

thinking can get you through rough times. It is not hard to believe that it can get you through every day, too. Just as Alex changed his attitude and his way of thinking, so can you. You can make positive thinking work in your life and start turning your bad situations into good ones. You can get favorable results and outcomes, too."

Conclusion

The influence of positive thinking is undeniable. Once you witness its impact, belief in its power becomes unwavering. Experiencing the transformative effect of positive thinking may leave you wondering how you ever managed without it.

Throughout this journey, you've gained insights into positive thinking—understanding its definition, exploring its facets, and unraveling the mechanics of how it operates. You've received valuable tips and guidance on transitioning into a positive thinker and leveraging this newfound perspective to reshape your life.

Positive thinking goes beyond merely adopting a can-do attitude; it necessitates a complete lifestyle shift. To fully embrace positive thinking, you must align every aspect of your life with this newfound mindset. The changes, both in yourself and those around you, will be profound.

Positive thinking is not a myth; it is a tangible

reality. The benefits are undeniable, and the transformation is within reach. It may require a focused effort to train your mind, but the rewards of integrating positive thinking into your life are well worth it.

Reflect on the story of John, who used the power of positive thinking to navigate through a challenging phase in his life. Additionally, be mindful of how excuses can hinder your progress toward becoming a positive thinker.

Hold onto the lessons learned, from thinking like a child to combating negative thoughts. This knowledge forms the foundation of your positive thinking journey.

As you move forward, don't let the insights gained fade away. This information is the cornerstone of your quest for positive thinking. Embrace the power of positive thinking, and don't shy away from the effort required. You have the potential to be a positive thinker and transform your life through this powerful mindset.

3

INNOVATIVE THINKING – COGNITIVE RESTRUCTURING

Innovative thinking is often misunderstood, as are the inventors who harness its power to bring groundbreaking ideas to life. Unfortunately, it's not uncommon for people to dismiss innovative thinking as a frivolous pursuit, but this perception couldn't be further from the truth.

Inventors, in particular, frequently find themselves labeled as eccentric or even considered a bit 'off their rocker,' especially if their inventions have not yet gained mainstream acceptance. History shows that many of the world's most renowned inventors were initially deemed insane—until their groundbreaking creations revolutionized the world.

Inventors are a unique breed. They are driven by their ideas and possess a singular focus on creating something extraordinary that can benefit society or transform the way we live. Their disregard for societal opinions sets them apart. Without inventors, our world would lack essential conveniences, from everyday items like toilet paper to transformative technologies such as computers. Inventions play a crucial role in shaping our daily existence.

What is Innovative Thinking?

Innovative thinking is characterized by the ability to transcend the visible and the obvious. It is a form of imagination, a creative and distinct way of looking at things. An innovative thinker possesses the capability to perceive the extraordinary within the ordinary.

At its core, innovation is closely tied to invention. It involves the capacity to generate ideas and concepts that have not been previously conceived. The mind of an innovative thinker operates differently from the more conventional, pragmatic mindset that characterizes the majority of individuals.

Considered a gift, innovative thinking is not universally inherent. While some people are naturally blessed with this ability, others must actively train their minds to think beyond conventional boundaries.

The application of innovative thinking extends to various facets of life. Whether it's creating a unique outfit, devising a groundbreaking business concept, or preparing an inventive dinner, innovative thinking opens up possibilities for creative solutions and novel ideas.

Myths Around Innovative Thinking

Misunderstandings and myths often surround innovative thinking, leading to misconceptions about its nature and effectiveness. One common misconception is the idea that innovative thinkers are perceived as strange or crazy. The stereotype of an inventor being scatterbrained and disorganized can discourage individuals from embracing innovative thinking. In reality, serious inventors may appear scatterbrained due to their intense focus on their work, not because of any inherent craziness.

Moreover, there is a misconception that innovative thinking is not productive, with people failing to recognize it as a valuable skill. Innovative thinking is a sought-after quality in the business world, as it enables individuals to generate new and useful ideas across various industries. It is a skill that can be honed and applied to create positive change.

Another misunderstanding is that innovative thinking has to be radical and groundbreaking. In truth, innovation can be simple, complex, or subtle. Not all innovative thinking requires a major upheaval; it can involve improving existing ideas or combining ideas from different sources to create something new.

Innovative thinking is not restricted to individuals with high intelligence or genius minds. While many renowned inventors were geniuses, innovative thinking is a skill that can be developed by anyone. It's not limited to those with high IQs or advanced degrees. The genius mind may be more open to new ideas, but everyone has the potential to be an innovative thinker.

Innovative thinking is not a highly structured process, and it does not adhere to specific rules. It often emerges from clutter and disorganization, and some of the greatest inventions have arisen from the depths of numerous ideas and failed attempts. Being highly organized is not a prerequisite for innovative thinking, and it can even thrive in chaotic environments.

Innovative thinking is not solely dependent on collaboration or structured brainstorming sessions. While listening to others may aid the process, innovative thinking is primarily an individual endeavor. Too many distractions or ideas from others can interrupt the creative thinking process, and some of the most famous inventors often work alone.

Although innovative thinking is often free-flowing, it can also be facilitated in structured environments, especially in business settings. Creating an environment that welcomes innovation is possible within the confines of a business structure.

There is a misconception that innovation has to be expensive and involve technology. In reality, innovative ideas can be simple and effective, requiring no advanced technology. Innovation is not limited to scientific breakthroughs and can encompass a wide range of ideas.

Failure is an integral part of innovation and should not be seen as a deterrent. Some of the best ideas have arisen from failures, and innovation is rooted in learning from those failures. It is not an immediate gratification process, and individuals seeking immediate rewards may be disappointed. Innovation often requires perseverance and a willingness to learn from failures over time.

Understanding innovative thinking is crucial to overcoming these myths and embracing the concept. It is a valuable skill that, when properly understood, can lead to positive change and creative solutions in various aspects of life.

How to Get Started with Innovative Thinking

Innovative thinking can be a natural gift for some, but for most people, it's a skill that needs to be cultivated and learned. Developing innovative thinking skills can be challenging, but recognizing certain abilities can make the process easier. Here are some skills that can be helpful in developing innovative thinking:

Seeing things differently: The ability to look at an object or concept from a unique perspective is a key aspect of innovative thinking. For example, looking at a pencil and seeing it as more than just a writing tool can be a starting point for innovative ideas.

Identifying areas for improvement: An innovative thinker can recognize aspects of existing ideas, products, or processes that can be enhanced or made better. This skill involves critical evaluation and a constant quest for improvement.

Analytical thinking: Innovative thinking often requires sifting through a vast amount of information to extract valuable insights. The ability to navigate through piles of data, separating the relevant from the irrelevant, is crucial for innovative thinking.

Commitment: Innovation is a process that demands dedication and perseverance. If you are someone who commits to a goal and doesn't easily give up, you possess a quality essential for innovative thinking.

Recognizing these skills within yourself is the first step toward becoming an innovative thinker. Even if you don't currently see yourself as an innovative thinker, understanding that these skills can be developed over time will empower you to nurture your creativity and come up with inventive ideas.

How It Works

The process of generating inventive ideas and inventions through innovative thinking follows a systematic path. While thinking, in its general form, may lack structure, there exists a framework that proves invaluable when engaging in innovative thinking. This structured approach ensures that ideas seamlessly evolve into tangible inventions.

Innovative thinking commences with a critical step – defining the situation. It requires a thorough examination of the working elements, understanding the necessities, and establishing the desired outcome. Essentially, you need to have a clear destination in mind, and a defined goal for your creative endeavors.

With the situation defined, the next step involves gathering information. Innovative thinking doesn't arise from thin air; it requires a foundation of knowledge. Exploring what others have attempted can help you avoid replicating mistakes and might unveil opportunities for improvement.

The heart of the innovative process is the brainstorming phase. During this stage, creativity knows no bounds, and any idea is worth exploring. Logic takes a back seat, as some of the most groundbreaking innovations arise from seemingly unrealistic concepts. Consider the example of cell phones, once deemed a far-fetched idea, now an integral part of daily life.

Following the brainstorming session, it's time to sift through the ideas. Weed out those that lack feasibility or compatibility, and compile a list of the most promising concepts. These selected ideas become the focus of the next stage.

Now, evaluate your list. Dive deeper into each idea, attempting to refine and develop them further. Certain ideas will naturally rise to the surface as the most viable, while others may fall by the wayside.

With a narrowed-down selection, the final solution begins to take shape. Define your ultimate solution and embark on the journey to bring it to life. This structured yet flexible approach to innovative thinking ensures that creativity flourishes while preventing great ideas from getting lost in the process."

How to Use Innovative Thinking

- Don't be afraid to be unconventional. Sometimes the best ideas come from thinking outside the norm. If everyone else is doing something one way, try thinking of a completely different approach.
- Embrace diversity of thought. Surround yourself with people from different backgrounds and

with different perspectives. This diversity can lead to a rich exchange of ideas and viewpoints that can spark innovative thinking.
- Practice mindfulness. Take time to be present in the moment and observe your surroundings. This can help you notice details and patterns that may lead to new ideas.
- Create a conducive environment. Ensure that your workspace is conducive to creative thinking. This could mean having a space that inspires you, is free from unnecessary distractions, and has tools or resources that stimulate your mind.
- Keep a journal. Write down your thoughts, ideas, and observations regularly. This can help you track your thought process, reflect on your ideas, and revisit them later for further development.
- Take risks. Don't be afraid to try something new or take a different path. Innovation often involves a degree of risk-taking. Learn from failures and view them as opportunities to grow.
- Challenge assumptions. Question assumptions about how things should be done. Just because something has always been done a certain way doesn't mean it can't be improved or done differently.
- Seek inspiration from diverse sources. Read books, attend lectures, watch documentaries, and expose yourself to a variety of subjects. Inspiration often comes from unexpected places.

Remember that innovative thinking is a skill that can be developed over time. It's about fostering a mindset that is open to new ideas, unafraid of failure, and willing to challenge the status quo. By incorporating these practices into your daily life, you can cultivate your innovative thinking abilities and apply them in various aspects of your personal and professional life.

Some Exercises

Embracing an innovative mindset is an enjoyable journey. It grants you the freedom to unleash your creativity without the constraints of conventional logic. During this process, you can let go of pre-established rules and explore your thoughts with unrestricted creativity.

To extract ideas and inventions through innovative thinking, it's essential to align your brain with this approach. Engaging in various exercises tailored to stimulate innovative thinking becomes the key to this alignment.

These exercises serve as catalysts, steering your mind away from its usual daily thinking patterns and encouraging it to delve into the realm of innovative possibilities.

Exercise 1:
We've all indulged in daydreaming at some point

in our lives. Take a moment now to immerse yourself in a daydream. Picture the life you desire, the goals you wish to achieve or imagine being in a place you've always wanted to visit.

To enhance your creativity, consider recording your daydream. Speak about the vivid images and scenarios that unfold in your mind. This recording can serve as a valuable resource, capturing imaginative ideas that may inspire you later on.

Daydreaming is a gateway to temporarily set aside practicalities and the routine of everyday life. It opens up a realm of possibilities, allowing your mind to explore and envision the extraordinary.

Exercise 2:

Free writing is a process where you sit down with a blank sheet of paper and jot down whatever crosses your mind. Grammar and structure are set aside; the goal is to express thoughts as they spontaneously emerge.

Initially, engaging in free writing may reveal the challenge of detaching from logical thinking. Your writing might lack creativity, and that's perfectly normal. Over time, you'll find it easier to tap into more imaginative and creative content. The primary objective is to understand your mind's workings.

After completing a free writing session, review your written words. Identify any intriguing or expandable ideas. If certain thoughts stand out, consider extracting them for further exploration through additional free writing sessions.

Exercise 3:

Children are exceptional innovative thinkers. As we mature, we often lose the sense of wonder and amazement for life that fuels innovative thinking. Spending a day with children can reignite that mindset and help you open your mind to creative thoughts.

Interacting with children can generate a multitude of ideas and evoke the childlike wonder within you. This experience enables you to recall your own perspective at that age, rekindling memories of how you viewed the world with curiosity and awe.

Exercise 4:

Engaging in activities you've never tried before or facing something that terrifies you can be transformative. Embracing novel experiences opens the door to learning more about yourself and the world around you.

Trying something new can range from exploring a different culture to undertaking daring endeavors, such as skydiving. Follow your instincts and venture into uncharted territory.

Embarking on new experiences triggers excitement and learning simultaneously, stimulating your brain in various ways. This stimulation prompts the release of triggers that can ignite creativity.

Exercise 5:

Playing music can activate the creative regions of your brain, facilitating the transition into the mental state required for innovative thinking.

Consider learning to play a musical instrument or exploring your vocal talents. Engaging in activities that stimulate the creative areas of your brain can help prime them for innovative thinking.

These exercises are valuable tools for developing innovative thinking skills. Feel free to experiment with all of them or select a few that resonate with you. Allowing yourself the space and time to engage in enjoyable activities like these exercises is crucial for fostering creativity and becoming an innovative thinker.

Passion

Passion plays a crucial role in innovative thinking. It's a powerful force that propels your ideas forward and convinces others of their value. Genuine passion for your innovative ideas is something that comes from the heart, an uncontrollable force that drives you to believe in and stand behind your concepts.

Developing passion is challenging, but when you feel an immediate and strong connection to an idea, it's a sign that it's worth pursuing. Passion is essential when communicating your innovative ideas to others.

It creates enthusiasm and conviction, making it difficult for people to dismiss or criticize your concept.

Persistence and passion work hand in hand in the realm of inventions and ideas. People may not be as receptive to your ideas as you are, so maintaining a strong drive is crucial. Keep pushing your idea, be prepared to answer questions, and stand firm behind your concept.

Without passion, it's easy to lose the fight and drive needed to bring your idea to fruition. Always remember the importance of passion in innovative thinking; it's the driving force that ensures your idea gets the recognition it deserves.

A Story

Here is a story about Emily. Emily is an innovative thinker. She has not always been, though. Emily found her innovative genius one day and has never let it go because of what it has done for her in her life.

Emily is an average woman. She has no extraordinary talents. She is not a genius. In fact, Emily never even went to college. What makes Emily different is that she is a great innovative thinker. The company Emily works for is a big-name company that usually only hires the best of the best. Her co-workers all have degrees from top universities. They were valedictorians and honor students. Emily does not feel out of place, though, because she knows she often produces work that they could only dream of producing. That is all because of her innovative thinking.

Emily was not born an innovative thinker. She had to work at it. It took her many years to perfect the art of innovative thinking. She had to do many exercises and had many failures.

Emily would spend a lot of her free time free writing and brainstorming. She also started to look at the world around her. She started to question everything. She started to look at everyday things and wonder how she could make them better.

One day she had a breakthrough and came up with an idea that changed her life forever. Emily invented a product that became very popular. She was recognized on national television, and she started getting phone calls from various companies who wanted her on their team.

Emily ended up at her current job, and she has never been happier. Her innovative thinking has led her to a life she could only dream of before.

Innovative thinking is amazing. It can work wonders in your life. All it takes is just getting started. You can make it work for you. You can build upon your innovative ideas and create something wonderful. You can use innovative thinking to make you stand out from the crowd.

Be like Emily and make your own future. Go out there and create, imagine, and invent. Use innovative thinking to guide you to the future you have only dreamed about.

Conclusion

You now possess a comprehensive understanding of innovative thinking. It's likely that your perspective on innovation has undergone a transformation, recognizing its profound impact on your life.

Having delved into the definition of innovative thinking, you're equipped to navigate common misconceptions that may deter individuals from embracing this powerful approach. This knowledge serves as motivation for you to adopt innovative thinking, appreciating its potential impact on your life.

You've familiarized yourself with exercises and techniques pivotal for cultivating innovative thinking. Understanding that innovative thinking is not confined to inventors or geniuses empowers you to envision its application in various aspects of your life.

Innovative thinking revolves around passion, requiring a deep commitment to stand behind unexplored ideas. This passion becomes instrumental in conveying the greatness of your ideas to others.

At its core, innovative thinking is about creativity. It's both constructive and liberating, enabling you to break free from self-imposed restrictions and explore the world with an open mind. Innovative thinking has played a pivotal role in shaping the modern world, giving rise to indispensable conveniences.

Crucially, innovative thinking is a skill that can be acquired. You don't need an innate talent; rather, you can train your brain to think innovatively with dedication and effort.

Recall the do's and don'ts to guide yourself in cultivating innovative thinking. While it may seem challenging, the journey toward becoming an innovative thinker lies within your grasp. The story of Sue exemplifies how one can overcome rational thoughts, allowing innovative thinking to pave the way to success.

You hold the key to unlocking innovative thinking in your life. Embrace the possibility of transforming your thought processes, knowing that innovative thinking can be seamlessly integrated into your regular life. It's time to dispel any fears and embark on the exciting journey of unleashing the power of innovative thinking!

4

CREATIVE THINKING

Creative thinking is the capacity to generate thoughts that are often unconventional and divergent. It revolves around the concept of venturing beyond conventional boundaries, encouraging thinking that is original and extends beyond the ordinary.

This skill is trainable, meaning that some individuals are naturally endowed with creative thinking abilities, while others need to actively cultivate this capacity. Regardless of one's starting point, anyone can develop into a proficient creative thinker with consistent effort and practice.

The power to incorporate creative thinking into your life lies within your hands. By embracing creative thinking, you have the potential to reshape not only your thoughts but also your entire world, fostering a transformative impact that lasts a lifetime.

What is Creative Thinking?

Creative thinking is a distinctive mental process that allows individuals to generate ideas and solutions beyond conventional boundaries. Unlike routine thinking, creative thinking involves exploring possibilities that extend outside the ordinary scope of thought.

For instance, consider the scenario of reimagining the use of a common product through creative thinking. While the product may have a conventional purpose, creative thinking encourages individuals to identify alternative applications, uncovering hidden potentials.

The development of creative thinking often entails acquiring specific skills and practicing various techniques. Unlike innate abilities, creative thinking is typically cultivated through deliberate effort, as it is not an automatic process.

As individuals enhance their creative thinking skills, they discover an ability to generate ideas rapidly. Creative thinkers tend to approach problems with a different mindset, opting for unconventional solutions rather than settling for the obvious answers.

Having a creative thinker in a group is advantageous, as they contribute multiple ideas, persist in finding solutions, and bring a unique perspective to problem-solving situations.

What Can Creative Thinking Do for You?

Creative thinking offers a plethora of advantages that significantly enhance an individual's value in the professional arena. This skill proves invaluable across diverse industries and businesses. The ability to think creatively empowers individuals to generate a multitude of ideas swiftly, a skill particularly advantageous in time-sensitive professions.

One of the standout benefits of creative thinking lies in its capacity to transform individuals into adept problem solvers. Creative thinkers possess the unique ability to devise innovative solutions that may elude others. Their knack for generating unconventional ideas contributes to effective problem resolution, making creative thinking a valuable asset across various professions.

Moreover, creative thinking imparts individuals with a fresh perspective, applicable to both professional and personal spheres. As individuals integrate creative thinking techniques into their daily activities, it becomes second nature, enabling them to approach tasks with a renewed and innovative mindset.

The impact of creative thinking extends to one's overall attitude and confidence. Embracing creative thinking cultivates self-assurance, allowing individuals to fulfill their true potential without doubting their abilities. This boost in morale serves as a catalyst for showcasing capabilities and achieving personal and professional goals.

Ultimately, creative thinking serves as a gateway to success and significant accomplishments. Creative thinkers are known for their dynamic approach, constantly innovating and staying at the forefront of their endeavors. Their ability to leverage creative thinking not only improves their lives but also positions them as valuable contributors, making it challenging to overlook their contributions. Embracing creative thinking is a transformative journey that can lead to a life of fulfillment and achievement.

How to Embrace Creative Thinking?

Adopting a creative thinking mindset is an exciting journey that allows you to explore the realms of imagination and fantasy. Creative thinking is not always grounded in rationality; in fact, many revolutionary ideas were once deemed crazy. The joy of creative thoughts lies in their uniqueness, often prompting others to wish they had conceived them.

One effective technique to cultivate creative thinking is through "thought experiments," a method famously used by Albert Einstein. Thought experiments stimulate the mind, encouraging individuals to surpass the obvious and delve into the creative.

Thought experiments are rooted in visualization, a crucial aspect of creative thinking. Visualization involves forming vivid mental images or imagining actions in the mind. It opens doors in the mind that may have remained closed.

To create thought experiments, consider the following steps:

Develop Thought-Evoking Questions: Form questions that challenge your thinking, ranging from answerable to rhetorical or even universal questions without a definitive answer.

Engage with Great Minds: Imagine having deep conversations with historical geniuses. Envision what questions you would ask and how they might respond.

Travel in Time or Dimensions: Explore alternate realities by imagining time travel or existence in another dimension. Visualize the surroundings, people, and aspects of life in these scenarios.

Contemplate Higher Beings: Think about the divine or higher beings, imagining the questions you would ask and their responses. Envision being in the presence of such power.

Experiment with Astral Projection: Study astral projection and attempt to project your consciousness out of your body into the astral plane.

Additionally, asking "what if" questions is a powerful creative thinking tool. Pose questions and explore multiple imaginative answers, delving deep into each possibility.

Other strategies to stimulate creative thinking include:

Breathing Exercises: Learn to use controlled breathing to relax and clear your mind, allowing creative thoughts to flow more freely.

Visualization Practice: Improve your ability to visualize by starting with simple mental images and progressing to more complex scenarios.

Gather Information: Learn about topics of interest to provide a foundation for creative thinking. Consider how your ideas can enhance or transform existing concepts.

Brainstorming with Others: Collaborate with friends to brainstorm ideas. Different perspectives can ignite creative thinking.

Role-Playing: Pretend to be someone else and think from their perspective. This helps break out of your own mindset.

Challenge Your Brain: Engage in puzzles and new activities to give your brain a workout, exposing yourself to diverse ideas.

By incorporating these techniques into your routine, you can train your mind to think creatively, leading to a richer and more imaginative thought process.

Some Examples

Engaging in thought experiments and utilizing "what if" techniques is an excellent way to expand your thinking and encourage creative thought. Here are some creative thinking exercises to try:

Living in a Virtual Reality World:
Imagine yourself residing in a virtual reality universe.
Outline a typical day, considering the virtual environment, interactions with programmed entities, simulated experiences, virtual sustenance, and any form of virtual society.

Day in the Life as a Historical Figure:
Envision a day as a prominent historical figure, contemplating thoughts, interactions with other historical figures, daily routines, communication, living arrangements, and any societal structures of that time.

Feel free to create your own thought experiments to stimulate your creative thinking actively.

Some "what if" ideas to consider:

What if you had the ability to time travel?
What if you woke up with a new superpower every day?
What if you could communicate with animals?
What if you discovered a parallel universe?
What if everyone spoke a different language?

Ponder age-old or rhetorical questions related to:
The concept of parallel universes
The existence of intelligent life beyond Earth
The possibility of time travel
The nature of consciousness

Explore common questions people often contemplate:

Is laughter the best medicine?
Can money buy happiness?
What defines true love?
If you could change one event in history, what would it be?
What if everyone in the world shared the same dream for a night?

For those interested in law, challenge your brain by delving into unsolved mysteries from various disciplines, stimulating creative thinking, and potentially contributing to solving real-world puzzles.

There are countless ways to stimulate your mind creatively—embrace free thinking and seek opportunities to challenge your brain actively.

Techniques

Step 1: Exploration

Embark on a comprehensive examination of the situation. Gather intricate details, asking questions to gain a deep understanding of the context. This phase involves uncovering the who, what, where, when, and how of the situation. By the end of the exploration, you should be able to articulate the situation, including any evident problems or challenges.

Step 2: Ideation

Enter the heart of creative thinking. Armed with knowledge about the situation, let your ideas flow freely. Ideation can take various forms, from verbalizing ideas to jotting them down on paper. The key is to ensure that all ideas are captured and documented during this uninhibited phase.

Step 3: Refinement

Now, with a collection of ideas, scrutinize and

refine them. Weed out impractical concepts and consider tweaking others for better effectiveness. This step involves fine-tuning your ideas, enhancing their feasibility and practicality.

Step 4: Synthesis

In the final step, narrow down your ideas further to identify one or two standout solutions. Review and evaluate these remaining ideas, delving into the details of how each solution will work and how it can be implemented.

Being a creative thinker requires the ability to think beyond structured frameworks. While these four steps provide a foundational structure, remember that creativity flourishes when given space for unrestricted exploration and thinking. Use these steps as a guide to navigate your creative thinking process effectively.

Steps to Becoming a Creative Thinker

So, you're eager to cultivate your creative thinking skills? Ready to unleash a torrent of innovative ideas whenever inspiration strikes? Let's delve into the steps you can take to become a creative thinker.

Start by embracing creativity in your everyday life. Consider taking up artistic hobbies, such as music or visual arts, as these activities stimulate the creative regions of the brain. Engaging in these pursuits allows your mind to break free from the constraints of rational thinking, paving the way for increased creativity. The more you immerse yourself in these activities, the more readily you can tap into your creative reserves.

Another effective approach is to engage in regular brainstorming sessions. Grab a pen and paper, and let your thoughts flow without inhibition. Avoid censoring yourself; instead, encourage the free expression of ideas. You might be surprised at the wealth of creativity you can uncover when reviewing your uncensored thoughts.

Experiment with thought exercises and explore "what if" scenarios, as suggested earlier. Dedicate time daily to these exercises, treating them with seriousness and commitment. Consistency is key to keeping your mind sharp and your creative juices flowing.

Becoming a creative thinker demands effort and commitment. Make it a daily practice, never slacking off if you genuinely aim to nurture a brain capable of creative thinking.

Anyone can adopt creative thinking, but it requires allowing your mind to wander and relinquishing strict control over your ideas. Creative thinking is about letting your thoughts flow freely and embracing a free-flowing mental process.

Practice regularly, letting your mind explore beyond the obvious and discover new ideas. Engage in activities like free writing, where you relinquish control over your thoughts. Challenge yourself with games that stimulate your mind and promote creative thinking. Try new things and step outside your comfort zone.

Becoming a creative thinker is simply a matter of determination. Once you commit to the journey, the only thing standing in your way is yourself. So, go ahead, embrace creativity, and let your innovative thoughts flourish.

A Story

Consider the story of Alex and Jordan as a vivid illustration of how creative thinking can significantly impact your career. Place yourself in their shoes and reflect on which character traits resonate more with you.

Alex, a confident individual with a business degree from a prestigious school, felt secure in their position at a great company. However, when a new employee, Jordan, joined with a reputation for genius, Alex's perspective shifted.

During a weekly meeting, the boss announced the need for a presentation to woo a potential client, scheduled for later in the week. Each team member was tasked with brainstorming ideas for the meeting later that afternoon.

At the follow-up meeting, Alex proposed a solid idea, earning praise from their boss. However, when it was Jordan's turn, they presented a brilliant, creative approach that left everyone in awe. The boss was so impressed that they entrusted Jordan with delivering the presentation.

Curious about Jordan's creative prowess, Alex engaged in a conversation. Jordan explained the principles of creative thinking, detailing how it had been instrumental in landing them the job. Intrigued, Alex decided to explore creative thinking techniques, regularly asking themselves "what if" questions and experimenting with thought exercises.

Soon, Alex and Jordan emerged as the top employees in the office, leveraging their creative thinking skills to climb the corporate ladder. Their collaboration was so successful that they eventually started their own company, achieving a net worth of over a million dollars within a year.

Reflect on your own situation—do you identify more with Jordan or Alex? Like them, you may not have initially recognized the significance of creative thinking. The story highlights that creative thinking can be a transformative skill, propelling individuals to success from the very beginning of their careers.

While book smarts and degrees are valuable, creative thinking can set you apart in the workplace. It's a skill that stimulates your brain and enables you to make a profound impact on your boss. Jordan's journey serves as a testament to the potential of creative thinking, showcasing how it can elevate you to become the star of your office. Embrace creative thinking, and you might find yourself on a path to success, just like Jordan.

Conclusion

Creative thinking is a versatile skill that can offer numerous benefits in various aspects of your life. The possibilities are vast, and embracing creative thinking can lead to personal and professional growth. After learning about creative thinking, you may now see its relevance to your life and its potential to enrich your experiences.

Becoming a creative thinker may require some effort and practice, especially if your mind isn't naturally inclined towards creativity. It involves looking beyond the obvious, thinking outside the box, and exploring alternative approaches to problems. Give yourself the freedom to daydream and let your thoughts flow without overthinking.

Don't be afraid to embrace unconventional ideas, and stand proudly behind your creative thoughts. Others may not always understand or appreciate your ideas, but that's okay. Creativity often challenges the norm, and being confident in your creative thinking can lead to remarkable outcomes.

Implement the advice and tips provided to kickstart your journey into creative thinking. Engage in thought experiments, ask "what if" questions regularly, and make creative thinking a habit. Train your brain to think freely, and over time, creative thinking will become second nature.

You hold the key to adopting creative thinking, and the commitment to letting go of rigid control is crucial. Remember, creative thinking is a powerful tool that can bring positive changes to your life. It allows you to view the world differently, grasp new concepts, and notice things that might have escaped your attention before.

In a fast-paced world, taking the time to slow down and appreciate the little wonders can be immensely rewarding. Creative thinking facilitates this by encouraging a shift in perspective. It's not just a skill; it's a way of experiencing life more fully. Don't hesitate to share your knowledge about creative thinking with others, just as Scott did in the example. Be a creative thinker and inspire those around you.

The decision to adopt creative thinking is yours alone, and the responsibility rests on your shoulders. Take this opportunity to reflect on what you've learned and consider incorporating creative thinking into your life. It's a gift and a skill that, once embraced, can open up new possibilities and make your journey more exciting and fulfilling. Start the journey of creative thinking today, and have fun training your mind to see the world in a different light. Don't walk away without giving creative thinking a chance to flourish in your life.

5

THE ART OF PROBLEM-SOLVING

We engage in problem-solving almost every day, often overlooking its significance. The true value and importance of problem-solving often go unrecognized. Regrettably, many people fail to acknowledge it as a skill, considering it a natural instinct.

In reality, problem-solving can be likened to an art form. This art of problem-solving is instilled in us from a young age, guiding us through life's challenges. It is a fundamental life skill, one that holds paramount importance and deserves serious consideration for optimal outcomes.

Viewing problem-solving through the lens of an art form can foster a greater appreciation for its nuances. Embracing problem-solving to its fullest potential allows for a profound understanding of its importance.

To truly grasp the essence of problem-solving, one must delve into it as both a skill and an art, unraveling its intricacies.

Why is Problem Solving Important

Problem-solving is an integral part of daily life, a skill that becomes indispensable in navigating the challenges that arise. Whether the issues are trivial or substantial, and whether the stakes involve life-and-death scenarios or maintaining one's sanity, the need for effective problem-solving is undeniable. For parents, this skill is particularly crucial, given the myriad of challenges that children present. Creative thinking often becomes a key component, as some problems necessitate innovative solutions that go beyond conventional methods.

In the realm of business, problems abound, demanding the application of adept problem-solving skills from employees. Complex issues may not succumb to simple problem-solving techniques, requiring a more nuanced approach.

As an individual, you encounter problems routinely, ranging from mundane inconveniences like flat tires to the complexities of rescuing a failing product line. Unbeknownst to many, you are, in essence, a problem solver, deploying your skills almost instinctively. However, this familiarity can sometimes lead to complacency, causing individuals to take their problem-solving abilities for granted.

The tendency to overlook the artistry inherent in problem-solving is common. Daily reliance on this skill might lead one to lean on established methods rather than exploring new, creative avenues. Reflecting on childhood approaches to problem-solving often reveals a more imaginative and creative mindset. However, as individuals mature, they tend to gravitate toward familiar, proven solutions rather than investing the time and effort required for more innovative problem-solving.

Acknowledging problem-solving as an art form can transform it from a mundane task into a captivating and fulfilling process. By recognizing the inherent creativity in problem-solving, individuals can elevate their skills, moving beyond routine solutions to embrace a more imaginative and effective problem-solving approach.

The Genius of Childlike Problem Solving

Children approach problem-solving with a distinctive mindset, showcasing a stark contrast to the problem-solving methods employed by adults. The divergence arises from the disparity in skill level and experience between the two groups. Understanding how children navigate problems can offer valuable insights.

A child, when faced with a problem, approaches it with a genuine openness that adults may lack. Unlike adults, who might harbor preconceived notions and view the problem as an inconvenience, children see it as an exciting challenge, akin to unraveling a great mystery.

Adults often carry a sense of frustration when unable to promptly resolve a problem. In contrast, a child views the situation as an opportunity for experimentation and learning. They exhibit relentless persistence, trying various approaches until they achieve success. In contrast, adults may be more inclined to give up or delegate the problem to someone else.

Children imbue problem-solving with wonder, amazement, and unwavering persistence, attributes that adults might overlook in their quest for expedient solutions. The disparity in problem-solving approaches underscores how adults often take this skill for granted, prioritizing the swift resolution of problems over the joy of overcoming challenges.

By embracing childlike problem-solving techniques, adults can infuse the process with a renewed sense of ease and enjoyment. Adopting a more open, persistent, and experimental mindset can transform problem-solving from a burdensome task into an artful and fulfilling endeavor.

Facets of Problem Solving

The art of problem-solving transcends mere reliance on the easiest solutions. It demands a thorough analysis of the problem, exploration of various solutions, and a conscious effort to find the most effective resolution. To truly understand the art of problem-solving, consider incorporating the following aspects into your approach the next time you encounter a problem, regardless of its scale.

Flexibility: Move beyond your comfort zone and resist the immediate urge to resort to familiar solutions. Be open to trying something different, as it may lead to innovative and effective outcomes.

Thoughtful Reflection: Take the time to step back and contemplate the situation before taking action. Engage in brainstorming to explore different approaches and consider your options thoroughly.

Inquisitive Mindset: Part of effective problem-solving involves generating new questions to address. By asking pertinent questions, you can uncover deeper insights and arrive at more comprehensive solutions.

Shift in Perspective: Look at the problem from a different angle. Challenge your natural inclinations and consider alternative viewpoints. Overcoming your initial thought patterns can lead to novel and effective problem-solving strategies.

Unconventional Thinking: Dare to propose solutions that may initially seem illogical or unconventional. Surprisingly, an unconventional idea might turn out to be the perfect resolution to your problem.

By incorporating these ideas into your problem-solving approach, you can transform the way you navigate challenges. Rather than opting for the most apparent conclusion, you'll develop the capacity to discern the ideal solution through thoughtful reflection and creative problem-solving. Remember that not every problem requires an immediate solution, and taking the time to employ the art of problem-solving can lead to more profound and effective outcomes.

Skills for Problem Solving

Problem-solving encompasses a variety of skills that are crucial for effective resolution. Here are some of the key skills:

Innovative Perspective: The capacity to view situations innovatively and explore beyond the apparent is crucial for effective problem-solving. Relying solely on the obvious may limit potential solutions. An innovative perspective allows for brainstorming and generating unique approaches to problems, fostering quick thinking beneficial in various professions.

Logical Analysis: While innovative thinking is essential, logical analysis aids in evaluating and selecting the most viable ideas. It enables you to distinguish between effective and ineffective solutions, leading to a more refined and effective resolution.

Impartial Approach: Approaching problems with an unbiased perspective and without preconceived notions is vital. An impartial approach allows consideration of various viewpoints and the exploration of different approaches, promoting a comprehensive problem-solving process.

Constructive Outlook: A constructive outlook significantly influences problem-solving success. Believing in your ability to solve a problem is a key factor. Approaching challenges with a constructive mindset enhances resilience and creativity in finding solutions.

These skills are foundational for effective problem-solving. If you possess these skills, consider refining and further developing them. If you don't, make a commitment to work on acquiring and honing these essential problem-solving abilities.

Moreover, it's important to recognize that there are additional skills beyond those listed that can contribute to effective problem-solving. Assess your existing skills and identify how each one can be applied to enhance your problem-solving capabilities. Conducting a thorough inventory of your skills will reveal valuable assets that can be utilized in various ways to improve your problem-solving proficiency.

Methods of Problem Solving

Numerous problem-solving approaches exist, and it's common for individuals to adopt a preferred method for addressing every challenge they encounter. However, sticking to a single method may not always be advantageous. Exploring various problem-solving techniques is crucial because what works best for one problem might differ from what's effective for another.

There are three primary avenues through which people tackle problems:

Inquisitive Inquiry: Some individuals navigate problems by posing questions. They examine the issue and ask 'what if' scenarios, contemplating potential outcomes. Through this inquisitive approach, they discern various possibilities, enabling them to identify the optimal solution for effectively resolving the problem.

Structured Methodology: For those who thrive

on organization or when dealing with intricate problems, a structured problem-solving process can be beneficial. This typically involves meticulous analysis of the problem, proposing diverse solutions, testing these solutions, and ultimately implementing the chosen resolution. It provides a systematic and disciplined approach to problem-solving.

Idea Generation: Creative problem solvers often turn to brainstorming. This entails sitting down and generating a multitude of potential solutions to the problem. Embracing innovative thinking and creativity allows individuals to explore unconventional ideas, potentially leading to unique and effective solutions.

While the ability to solve problems is inherent, the efficacy of problem-solving lies in one's approach. Embracing a willingness to experiment with different methods and approaches is key. This flexibility allows for the generation of multiple solution options, increasing the likelihood of discovering the most effective resolution.

Make Solving Problems Practical

Once you delve deeper into problem-solving, moving beyond its fundamental necessity, you can truly appreciate and embrace it as an art form.

This deeper understanding empowers you to elevate

your problem-solving skills and become a master at it. You'll be recognized as the go-to person for solutions, with others seeking your advice and assistance when challenges arise.

With this mastery, you not only navigate problems effectively but also proactively address potential issues. The art of problem-solving becomes an integral part of your life, and you'll discover that it is indispensable.

Viewing problem-solving through this different lens transforms your approach. Instead of dreading challenges, you embrace them, actively working toward finding solutions. Beyond addressing issues, this mindset contributes to a smoother life, making it easier to handle adversity. Over time, you'll experience an enhanced sense of self and overall happiness.

Problem-solving is not merely a skill; it's an art that has the potential to positively change your life. The ability to swiftly and efficiently solve problems is a unique trait, not everyone possesses.

While some may crumble in the face of challenges, you can rise above by effectively applying problem-solving methods. Maintaining a calm and level-headed demeanor allows you to navigate toward optimal solutions.

Focus on the Positive

Developing a positive mindset is crucial for becoming an effective problem solver. Approaching problem-solving with optimism is a key element for success.

Often, people enter into problem-solving with preconceived notions that the issue is insurmountable. Believing you can't accomplish something sets you up for failure. Instead, foster a positive mindset, approaching problems with the conviction that you can overcome them effortlessly.

A positive attitude is synonymous with keeping your mind open, a vital aspect of effective problem-solving. With a can-do attitude, you prevent frustration from taking over easily. This mindset encourages the free flow of ideas, making you more inclined to explore multiple solutions.

Your attitude might be the primary obstacle hindering your problem-solving abilities. Reflect on how you typically approach problems. If negativity dominates your mindset, simply altering your attitude can significantly enhance your problem-solving skills.

Take the initiative to infuse positivity into your problem-solving approach. Convince yourself that you can tackle the problem successfully. Resist the pull towards negativity.

Remember, a positive attitude plays a substantial role in problem-solving. Don't underestimate the influence your mindset can have. Keep it positive for optimal results.

Here is an Example

Understanding how children approach problem-solving compared to adults is crucial, as adults tend to lose some of the valuable problem-solving skills they had in childhood.

One reason for this shift is the increased emphasis on logic in adulthood. Adults often prefer direct, proven solutions over creative approaches. They may avoid experimentation and opt for what they believe will work, leading to frustration if their chosen method fails.

Children, on the other hand, approach problems differently. Consider the following scenario to illustrate the distinct approaches of an adult (Kevin) and a child (Kevin Junior) facing the challenge of setting up a video game system:

Situation: Kevin and his son, Kevin Junior, receive a video game system to connect to a television. Neither has directions or prior experience.

Kevin's Approach:
Kevin methodically lays out all the cords and examines each piece. He selects what seems like the correct cord for the TV connection, hooks everything up, but the system doesn't work. After repeated attempts, frustration sets in, and he contemplates if the system is faulty.

Junior's Approach:

Junior immediately starts connecting cords. Realizing he forgot to plug in the system, he does so, but the TV still doesn't display anything. Instead of giving up, he experiments with the television settings, changing the channel, and successfully gets the system working.

Kevin's quick frustration led him to miss the obvious step of plugging in the system, and he was ready to make excuses. In contrast, Junior persisted, experimented, and found success without missing the obvious.

Kevin's Approach:

1. **Systematic Analysis:** Kevin starts by laying out all the cords and pieces systematically. This demonstrates a methodical and organized approach to problem-solving.
2. **Logical Deduction:** Kevin attempts to deduce the correct cord by examining each piece. His reliance on logic is evident, seeking a straightforward solution based on observation.
3. **Repetition of Failed Method:** When the system doesn't work initially, Kevin repeats the same method multiple times. This reflects a persistence in sticking to a chosen approach, even in the face of failure.

4. **Frustration and Quick Conclusions:** Faced with repeated failures, Kevin becomes frustrated and quickly concludes that the system might be broken. This shows a tendency to give up easily and attribute the problem to external factors.

Junior's Approach:

1. **Immediate Action:** Junior jumps right in, connecting cords without a systematic analysis. This indicates a willingness to take immediate action, even without a clear plan.
2. **Realization and Adaptation:** Recognizing the omission of plugging in the system, Junior adapts quickly by addressing the missing step. This demonstrates flexibility and adaptability in response to new information.
3. **Experimentation:** Instead of repeating the same steps, Junior experiments by adjusting the television settings. This creative and experimental approach allows him to discover the solution through trial and error.
4. **Persistence and Focus:** Junior persists in finding a solution, staying focused on the problem at hand. He doesn't get discouraged by initial failures and remains committed to solving the problem.

Comparison:
- **Creativity vs. Logic:** Junior's approach is more creative, involving experimentation and adaptation, while Kevin relies on a logical deduction process.
- **Flexibility vs. Rigidity:** Junior's flexibility in trying new things contrasts with Kevin 's rigid adherence to a method that has already proven unsuccessful.
- **Persistence vs. Frustration:** Junior's persistence in the face of challenges contrasts sharply with Kevin 's frustration and quick inclination to give up.

In summary, Kevin 's approach is characterized by systematic analysis, logical deduction, repetition, and quick frustration. In contrast, Junior's approach involves immediate action, realization, experimentation, and persistence. Emulating Junior's blend of creativity, flexibility, and persistence can enhance problem-solving skills by encouraging adaptability and a positive mindset.

This example highlights the difference in problem-solving approaches. While Kevin might have eventually figured it out, Junior's persistence and willingness to experiment led to a quicker and more successful resolution. Emulating Junior's approach, characterized by resilience and experimentation, can enhance problem-solving skills in adults.

Conclusion

Solving problems is an art that demands a genuinely creative mind. It entails cultivating creative thinking, a skill that can be acquired. This art form deserves high regard, emphasizing the need to approach problem-solving seriously but with a balanced perspective.

As demonstrated, adults often lose their problem-solving prowess by becoming too hasty in completing tasks. They forego the crucial element of thoughtful consideration. Problem-solving necessitates more than merely addressing the obvious; it requires contemplating the less apparent aspects.

Contrastingly, children excel as problem solvers because of their fearlessness in attempting various approaches. They invest time and effort without concern for external judgments, viewing problem-solving as an enjoyable challenge rather than a tedious task.

Unfortunately, adults often prefer surrendering rather than exerting effort. They perceive problem-solving as an unwelcome chore, failing to recognize its potential for excitement and fulfillment. Shifting this perspective involves revisiting the approach to problems, reminiscent of a child's mindset.

Approaching problems with a positive attitude is imperative. Believing in one's problem-solving abilities and avoiding immediate thoughts of difficulty are crucial. Self-doubt can undermine even the most proficient problem-solving efforts. The mind's power is immense—believing in your capability significantly influences your outcomes.

The mindset of "mind over matter" holds true. Trying various strategies and actively working toward a solution, rather than passively waiting for clarity, is essential. Problem-solving is an innate skill, and challenges, big or small, are inevitable. Being well-prepared for unexpected problems is crucial, and becoming an adept problem solver is a logical and valuable pursuit.

Becoming a proficient problem solver is an asset, making you an invaluable presence in any situation. Transform into the person who approaches complex issues with creativity and delivers effective solutions. Refrain from being the one who shies away or makes excuses. Maintain a positive outlook, reminiscent of Junior in the earlier example, who persisted and experimented until he succeeded.

Embrace the art of problem-solving in your life, witnessing its effectiveness. Abandon the habit of relinquishing challenges to others; instead, take charge and solve your problems. The satisfaction and personal growth that result will undoubtedly be rewarding.

www.ingramcontent.com/pod-product-compliance
Lightning Source LLC
Chambersburg PA
CBHW071023080526
44587CB00015B/2469